Teaching Peer Support for Caring and Cooperation

A six-step method

Talk Time

Ruth MacConville and Tina Rae

P·C·P

Paul Chapman
Publishing

© Dr Ruth MacConville and Tina Rae 2006

First published 2006

Paul Chapman Publishing
A SAGE Publications Company
1 Oliver's Yard
55 City Road
London EC1Y 1SP

SAGE Publications Inc.
2455 Teller Road
Thousand Oaks, California 91320

SAGE Publications India Pvt Ltd.
B-42, Panchsheel Enclave
Post Box 4109
New Delhi 110 017

www.luckyduck.co.uk

Commissioning Editor: George Robinson
Editorial Team: Mel Maines, Sarah Lynch, Wendy Ogden
Designer: Jess Wright

**A catalogue record for this book is available from the British Library
Library of Congress Control Number 2005907301**

ISBN 13 978-1-4129-1204-4
ISBN 10 1-4129-1204-0

Printed on paper from sustainable resources

Printed in Great Britain by The Cromwell Press Ltd, Trowbridge, Wiltshire

Te   for

C   on

A Lucky Duck Book

Contents

How to use the CD-ROM

The CD-ROM contains PDF files, labelled 'Worksheets.pdf' which consists of worksheets for each lesson in this resource. You will need Acrobat Reader version 3 or higher to view and print these resources.

To photocopy the worksheets directly from this book, set your photocopier to enlarge by 125% and align the edge of the page to be copied against the leading edge of the copier glass (usually indicated by an arrow).

Introduction and Background

Children understand children and also take the time to listen to each other (Tyrell, 2002). This is probably the most important reason why there has been such an increase in peer support programmes recently. This book is aimed at all those who are committed to the development of peer support programmes in schools. Most primary schools are now doing a great deal to promote social, emotional and behavioural skills (SEBS) either through the whole school environment or specifically through the framework of the National Healthy School Standard or the Personal Social Health Education (PHSE) Citizenship curriculum. Peer support programmes take this agenda an important step further by challenging the notion of the teacher as the source and mediator of knowledge thus enabling pupils to develop a sense of responsibility for themselves and for each other and thus have a real impact upon their school. Peer support programmes provide an opportunity for pupils to play an active part in real decision making about issues which interest them and in a very real and immediate way prepare pupils to be responsible citizens of the future. The benefits of peer support programmes are neatly summarised by Cowie and Wallace (2000) who suggest that they benefit children who have family and social problems, improve the general climate of the school and give social skills training to the peer supporters themselves.

In developing this programme, we have aimed to harness the skills of those pupils who are well accepted and liked within the school community in order to include others who may have low social status whilst also promoting a more positive and pro-social inclusive culture throughout the school community.

What is culture? It is a very difficult word to define. Culture can be described as the characteristic atmosphere or 'personality' of a community. Certainly each school has its own particular 'personality' or atmosphere which is tangible to visitors. In devising this programme we have set out to create a peer support programme which can transform the culture of a school by generating a spirit of acceptance, openness and geniality throughout its community.

This programme has been inspired by the Circle of Friends approach which is probably one of the best known peer support programmes. Circle of Friends, sometimes known as Circle of Support, is a powerful tool for inclusion which was originally developed by Forest (et al, 1993) in North America. The values that underpin the Circle of Friends approach are, 'full inclusion for all; the belief that there is not social justice until each belongs and has an equal place in our schools and communities,' (Newton and Wilson, 1999, p 5). The Circle of Friends approach works by developing a support network around individuals in the school community who are experiencing social difficulties often due to a specific disability, difference or behaviour. Volunteers from the peer group meet regularly with the target pupil therefore ensuring that relationships are built around him/her. The group also problem solves with the target pupil in order to address any social difficulties that she may be experiencing in school. We have used this approach to great effect in many schools in order to ensure the inclusion of individual pupils. Newton and Wilson (1999) emphasise that the process of creating a circle of friends is a simple one, 'No complex psychological theories are necessary. The message is also a simple one – relationships are what matter most' (p 13). Based on our experience of working with Circles of Friends in schools we have developed this programme.

Talk Time builds on the simple message of Circle of Friends that relationships are what matter most and emphasises that relationships happen through listening and talking to each other. We reasoned that if Circle of Friends can enhance the inclusion of individual pupils then a similar process structured in a slightly different way could be used to enhance the social climate of the classroom and create a more positive and cooperative working environment.

The programme employs the basic framework of Circle of Friends but targets a wider number of pupils and avoids what in our experience can sometimes be a difficulty with Circle of Friends which is the focus on an individual pupil, his social difficulties and the inevitable discussion about the target pupil in their absence. In our experience this is not acceptable to some pupils and in fact may heighten their social isolation. Talk Time overcomes the difficulties associated with Circle of Friends by creating a group of pupils who meet together to offer mutual support to each other without a focus on an individual pupil. Pupils do not volunteer to join the group but are carefully selected for the programme. The group includes pupils who have high social status and others who may have low social status within the peer group.

Talk Time is a process of pupils talking and listening to each other with a sense of purpose; hence its name. The focus throughout the programme is on developing language as a tool for thinking collectively and on co-reasoning. In developing it we have been influenced by Mercer's notion of exploratory talk:

> ...in which partners engage critically but constructively with each other's ideas. Relevant information is offered for joint consideration. Proposals may be challenged, and counter challenged, but if so reasons are given and alternatives are offered. Agreement is sought on the basis of joint progress.

(Mercer, 2000, p 153)

This programme is intended to be a continuous conversation that is started in the group setting. Here the selected pupils are encouraged to find and build on a common sense of values and worth that continues in the school. Just as Circle of Friends emphasises that relationships are what matter most, this book is also about the importance of relationships. The aim is to encourage the group members to talk to each other and make that conversation into one that develops over time and is increasingly shared with others in order to promote social growth within the school community. The group becomes the area of common ground between the selected pupils which is built up during each of the meetings. The more values and strategies are shared between the pupils the more a sense of community develops. What holds the intervention together is a structured way of doing things; the weekly meetings have a set routine, focusing on positive solutions.

Throughout this book we have referred to the group leader as 'facilitator'. The facilitator may be a teacher, learning mentor, school counsellor and so on. What is important is that who ever leads the group provides structure and leadership and at the same time allows the pupils to find their own way of dealing with challenging situations, does not gloss over what are important issues to the pupils and ensures that the group is not dependent on the adult to solve their problems. The facilitator must ensure that the pupils work well as a team, think creatively and solve problems cooperatively.

Talk Time as an intervention initially targets the whole class and aims to identify pupils who are already well accepted and liked by their peer group and also those who have low social status. It is important to emphasise from the outset that the activities that are used to assess each individual pupils' social acceptance within the class are completed individually and in confidence. The selected pupils (usually between 8 – 12 pupils) who are chosen to form the group then work cohesively as a team. No distinction is made between those pupils who already have high social acceptance and those who are not so well accepted by their peers. The group meetings provide a context in which the selected pupils can enhance their own personal levels of social acceptance, create a more positive social climate and consequently a more cooperative working climate within the classroom. Pupils who already have high social status within the peer group will benefit by active involvement in a structured group and from active involvement in what Resnick (1987) called 'High Quality Thinking'. Solutions are not fully known in advance or obvious from a single viewpoint, they involve judgement and interpretation and may offer more than one solution to a problem. High Quality Thinking may involve uncertainty and requires mental effort.

The careful selection of pupils to form the group is sometimes called sociometric grouping and works by providing the opportunity for a socially diverse group of pupils to work together. The work of Duck (1991) illustrates that grouping pupils according to their social status rather than relying on random groupings provides opportunities for pupils who would not usually interact with each other to get along together. Pupils work outside their friendship groups and this type of grouping helps reduce prejudice and fosters trust across gender and ethnic groups as well as including neglected or rejected pupils into the group. Proximity is an important antecedent of friendship; thus the more often pupils interact the more likely they are to become friends.

As pupils move through Key Stages 2 and 3 they become increasingly more able to view things from another's point of view and gain in their ability to empathise with others. The development of empathy depends on experience. Younger children will begin to appreciate new perspectives most similar to their own and developing their empathy involves providing relevant social experiences and reflecting upon them in a structured way. The development of empathy is accelerated by providing pupils with exposure to reasoning at one level above the stage the pupil is using. Throughout the programme pupils have opportunities to hear the social reasoning of their peers and develop a solution focused approach to the social challenges that arise. The programme aims to ultimately change the school from within by utilising the positive skills and interpersonal qualities that already exist within the peer group to make the class and then ultimately the school a more socially inclusive environment. The programme does not therefore involve a 'deficit' model for 'fixing' the needs of one child but rather seeks to develop a tool to promote inclusion and the ethos necessary to enable inclusion to exist. This is vital, given that inclusive education is rightly deemed to be a human right (Centre for Studies on Inclusive Education, 1998).

The programme can be used to develop a sense of community in the class and the school. It is an important tool for enhancing the social cohesion of pupils and for ensuring that a class gels. It can be used for ensuring pupils experience a smooth transition from primary to high school. At points of transition pupils need to find their own feet but some also need a supporting hand which the programme can provide. In our experience it is particularly useful to use with Year 7 pupils in the second half of the autumn term. This is the time when they have begun to find their feet within a new class or year group but may need an additional boost in building group cohesiveness and facilitating relationships.

Main aims of the approach

The main aims of the approach are:

- to increase the level of acceptance and inclusion of pupils who are currently deemed to be excluded from the peer group

- to harness and further develop the skills of pupils who are already considered to be highly skilled in terms of providing friendship and support to others

- to encourage staff to reflect upon their own views and practices in order to develop more inclusive approaches, resources and policies

- to impact positively upon whole-school structures and systems via encouraging a review by the whole school community as to how these can be made more inclusive

- to promote a cultured ethos of social support which encourages all staff and pupils to utilise and develop their own skills in terms of valuing and supporting others

- to encourage the continued and on-going use of 'support teams' in order to ensure the inclusion of all pupils in the school context

- to further develop the social and emotional skills of those pupils identified as members of the group, for example, the ability to listen, to reflect, to evaluate, to empathise, to problem-solve, to understand, identify and cope effectively with feelings (of self and others).

The success of the intervention can and should be measured by these aims.

The Structure of the Programme

Whole-school approach

The first step in setting up is to give the whole staff a short introduction to the programme and then explain the rationale for setting it up in the school. It is important that all staff understand the philosophy and aims which underpin the intervention. In our experience in order for the intervention to succeed it is necessary to have the support and understanding of all staff. Perhaps the most efficient way of ensuring that a whole-school approach is adopted is by distributing an information sheet to staff and then being available at a staff meeting or briefing to answer any questions staff may have about the programme. An example of an information sheet for staff can be found in Appendix 1.

Parents/carers

A second essential step in setting up the programme is contacting parents/carers. It is essential that they are fully informed about the programme well before it is introduced to the class. An example of the letter that could be sent can be found in Appendix 2.

Note: the number of group sessions that are held are at the discretion of the facilitator, however it is important to ensure that the group members, as far as possible, are aware of how many sessions they will be asked to attend.

The intervention is set out in a series of six steps as follows:

Step 1: The Whole Class Session

The purpose of this session is:

- to introduce the class to the Talk Time programme

- to identify the pupils who may most usefully be included in the group by way of two activities, the Relationship Circles and the Friendship Quiz

- to encourage the class to understand and begin to explore the link between feelings and behaviour, and how underlying emotional needs maybe expressed through behaviour.

At the end of the session the facilitator assesses the pupils' responses to the Relationship Circles and the Friendship Quiz and decides on the basis of these activities and his prior knowledge of the pupils who will be asked to join the group. The facilitator then keeps the completed Relationship Circles and Friendship Quiz worksheets and asks the pupils to repeat both activities at the end of the programme. Changes to the pupils' responses on these activities will help to evaluate its success. The use of the Friendship Quiz and the Relationship Circles as both tools for assessment and to evaluate pupil progress are explained in the Step 1 section.

Step 2: Setting up the Group

Once the group members (usually between 8 – 12 pupils) have been identified and made a commitment to participate, the first meeting will need to include a more in-depth introduction to the programme. During this session the facilitator will need to:

- introduce the pupils to the purpose and nature of the group
- encourage the pupils to set and agree a series of group rules in order to protect and ensure the security of the group
- encourage the pupils to choose a group name and logo
- agree how to record the work done in the group
- introduce the pupils to the focus activity and the Take Home Activity.

Step 3: Focus on Positive Behaviours

Group rules are reinforced at the start of the second group session. Pupils then focus on the skills and behaviours that enable us to get along with each other. It is important that the facilitator emphasises to the group that throughout the group discussions they should think in terms of behaviours and skills and always remember to keep names confidential. Pupils complete the Brainstorming sheets 'What makes others like us?' and 'Why are some people less easy to get along with?' The final Take Home Activity requires pupils to each begin to identify a personal target that they would like to achieve in order to improve their ability to get along with others. Pupils are encouraged to come prepared with a mental list for the start of the next session.

Step 4: Taking Action

During this session the pupils begin to identify the personal areas of change that they would each like to accomplish. Time in the group is spent focusing on each pupil and encouraging them to articulate their goals and targets. The pupils then consider how they might be able to support each other and enable each other to achieve their goals. Pupils each complete a Target sheet for themselves and also identify how they will actively support one other pupil in the group during the coming week. There is also the opportunity for the group members to discuss their concerns and for the facilitator to reinforce the central ethos and philosophy underpinning the intervention.

Step 5: Reflecting and Setting Targets

Pupils make use of a Scaling Activity in order to measure progress in terms of meeting their personal targets and also report back on how they have supported the targets of other pupils in the group. There is the opportunity to reflect upon why things may have gone well or not so well and to identify future action, strategies and targets. The pupils are encouraged to work together as a team in order to problem-solve any difficulties that they may have encountered over the week and to agree a support network for the coming week. Solution focused strategies are used throughout the sessions.

Step 6: Evaluation

The final session provides pupils with the opportunity to evaluate the work that they have done in the sessions. A final Scaling Activity and Reflect and Review sheets are completed by each member of the circle. The brainstorming activity during the final session encourages the pupils to articulate the range of skills, strategies and ideas that they have learnt from the sessions. This allows for the positive and pro-social nature of the work to be celebrated. The Friendship Quiz and Relationship Circles can be repeated if this is seen as a useful strategy to compare any changes over the programme. Finally, the facilitator presents certificates of participation to each pupil and time is allocated to celebrating successes, that is, with appropriate refreshments!

Included at each step are outlines of the sessions and clear guidelines as to how to deliver and guide the activities. At the end of each section is a list of resources that the facilitator will require to lead the session. Photocopiable sheets for the pupils' activities are provided at the end of each section.

Guidelines for Facilitators

Confidentiality

It is essential that pupils who participate in the programme feel secure in the knowledge that their contributions and all discussion within the group will be treated with respect and in confidence both by the facilitator and by the other pupils at all times, both inside and outside the group. When initially setting up the group and agreeing a set of rules, the issue of confidentiality needs to be stressed. The facilitator will need to emphasise that talking about the group and divulging other's views or problems outside the sessions would be a betrayal of trust and damage the confidence and self-esteem of all those who are involved in the group. The facilitator will need to make it clear to the pupils that if anyone of them breaks the confidentiality rule he/she will as a matter of consequence be asked to leave the group.

Brainstorm

Each session of the programme including the initial whole class session involves a brainstorm component. The question or issue to be discussed can be written up onto a flipchart so as to focus the pupils' attention. The pupils' responses can also be recorded by the facilitator on the flipchart. It will be important to encourage the pupils to contribute their ideas as this gives some indication as to their understanding of the concepts being addressed in the session. However, pupils should be allowed to pass, that is, not contribute, if they feel so inclined.

Solution focused approach (Rhodes and Ajmal, 1995)

This approach focuses upon the development of solutions as opposed to the exploration of problems. It ensures that individuals are recognised as more than the sum of their problems and are given full credit for their achievements. The facilitator and pupils focus on what is working so that a context of strength is created. Problem talk is turned into solution talk enabling seemingly 'stuck' situations to become 'unstuck'. Strategies which the facilitator may find useful include:

- Miracle Question: pupils are required to imagine themselves in a situation in which their negative feelings and problems are solved. The question may be presented in the following way:

  'Imagine that you go to bed tonight and a miracle happens!

  All your problems and difficulties are solved. You wake up to the perfect day both at home and at school. What is different? Talk through what would happen on this ideal day.'

  The reason behind presenting this Miracle Question is to enable the pupils to talk about life without the problem' and begin to formulate suggestions and ideas as to how they might begin to make changes. They should also be more able to identify and formulate appropriate and achievable personal goals.

- Reframing: this process involves the facilitator helping the pupil to find another way of looking at a situation which will hopefully increase the chances of the pupil overcoming the problem.

- Scaling Activity: this aims to provide a visual image by which pupils can clarify where they feel they 'are at' and where and how they would like to move on from this point. Scaling is a useful strategy for encouraging pupils who have a limited vocabulary to express themselves. When words fail, numbers can come to the rescue. Pupils are encouraged to rate themselves on a scale of 0-10. A rating such as 0 would indicate that the pupil feels extremely negative about life. A rating of 5 would indicate that they feel generally OK and recognise the need to make improvements. A rating of 10 would imply that things couldn't be better. The rating scale should be explained to the pupils as they begin to identify their targets. Once a rating has been recorded pupils should be encourage to reflect upon the following three questions:

    1. Why am I where I am on the scale?

    2. Where would I like to be?

    3. How can I get there, that is, what do my own personal targets have to be?

Target setting

During each session the pupils spend time focusing on the targets that they would like to achieve. A worksheet for this process is provided. The activity requires the pupils to reflect upon the development of their skills and to set personal targets for which they are solely responsible. Pupils choose one behaviour that they would like to work on and with the help of the other pupils in the group formulate a specific, personal target. Some pupils will change their targets on a weekly basis, whilst others may need to keep the same target for a few weeks. Although the pupils play an important role in supporting each other in the setting of realistic targets the facilitator has a critical role in overseeing and monitoring the process and also in supporting the pupils and in valuing their achievements.

Recording the sessions

Pupils will need to make their own decisions regarding the recording of work and group discussions. Some may wish to keep a personalised record of work whilst also contributing to a group record book whilst other groups may simply opt to maintain the one collective record. It is entirely up to them! Most important is that all their work and contributions to the process are valued and that a record of the sessions is maintained and well-presented. A well-presented record will reinforce both the value of the work and each participant's self-esteem.

Frequently Asked Questions

1. What happens if a member of the group decides they no longer wish to participate?

This usually doesn't arise at all as pupils are generally expected to understand at the outset that they are making a commitment to the group for its duration. However, if a pupil does decide that they no longer wish to participate either because they are experiencing a high level of stress or personal problems or because they may feel unsuited to such a role at the time, then they need to be given the option to withdraw. It is unproductive to ask someone to participate against their will. This will simply have a negative impact upon the work of the group as a whole – where there's no will there's no way! What will, however, need to be reinforced is the importance of the confidentiality rule and the fact that this still applies if a member leaves the group or when the group itself is finally disbanded.

2. Can other pupils join the group at a later date?

The group should consist of the same members from start to finish. As the pupils are carefully selected to take part in the programme there is the danger that an additional pupil will disturb the dynamics of the group. Overall we would not recommend additions throughout the intervention as this might have the detrimental effect of unfocusing the group and cause problems in terms of managing targets and allocating responsibilities.

3. What do you do if parents/carers refuse permission for their child to be a part of the group?

Ask again. We would suggest that if the process and its benefits are described accurately then parents/carers will definitely want their children to participate. Accurate knowledge of the process involved and on-going access to the facilitator will usually dispel any myths or fears which may have surrounded the programme. However, should the parents/carers maintain this stance, there is little that can be done. No intervention of this kind can or should take place without the full knowledge and agreement of the parents/carers.

4. Isn't there a danger that the facilitator's selection of group members will perpetuate their existing preferences?

Only if the facilitator is entirely unreflective, blinkered and emotionally illiterate. If this were the case, then she would hardly be an appropriate person to set up and run an intervention that demands the opposite of all of these qualities. Unlike the original Circle of Friends approach, which can make use of a range of selection methods, for example, random selection, pupil, teacher or facilitator selection or a mix of the last three, group members are selected for a range of specific inter and intra personal qualities which are identified via the initial whole-class session's activities (Relationship Circles and Friendship Quiz) and through on-going observation and discussion amongst involved staff. The aim is to identify those pupils who already have the necessary skills to support others and those who may benefit from participating in a group process that will help to further promote their less evident skills and allow them to achieve more of their potential in this area. Harnessing the power of such a group can have far reaching effects upon the peer group as a whole – not just the smaller group of pupils. The focus is on creating an ethos of support, tolerance, understanding, empathy and inclusion amongst the whole peer group. The group members need to be 'role models' and impact upon how the wider group functions. This is not the same as being a member of a small group of peers who support one individual (and, in our view, should therefore be chosen by that individual). This intervention is wider reaching and consequently demands a facilitator selection process.

5. Do you need to set a time limit?

We consider that it is important for the group members to have an idea as to how long they are expected to commit themselves to this programme. Usually, somewhere in the region of 8-10 weeks tends to be a useful period in which the pupils can actually experience and implement the desired changes. It is sensible to set an 'end' date to ensure a proper evaluation and closure of the group. The need for another group should be apparent at the final evaluation meeting. School based staff, the facilitator and pupils may well decide that Talk Time needs to continue and become part of the whole-school inclusion policy and practice. We hope so!

6. What if group members are frequently absent?

Ultimately, this will result in the group member(s) in question being very much 'left out' of the process, which really is dependent on a regular commitment in order to ensure a cohesive team approach. The process of reflection, evaluation and target setting should occur within the group context, ensuring that all participants' views are considered and tasks are allocated by agreement. Continual absences would clearly mitigate against the success of this process. The facilitator would need to consult with members of the group and the frequently absent member(s) in order to talk through the situation and attempt to come to some agreement as to the way forward. In our experience a group member who is absent on one or two occasions during a programme can be managed; however, any greater level of absence has unfortunately not contributed to viable working conditions for the group and this has usually resulted in the frequently absent pupil withdrawing from the programme.

7. How would you set about enlisting staff support for the programme?

We have found that staff are very willing to support the programme if they have been made fully aware of its purpose and if there is continual liaison and feedback to staff as to how the intervention is progressing. This demands a great deal of sensitivity, effort and time on the part of the facilitator. We have found that if staff feel included in the process via on-going dialogue with the facilitator, then this will create and maintain a positive view of the programme and mitigate against any form of negativity. Just as the intervention aims to include the pupils, it should also aim to include staff and to increase their knowledge of inclusive practices and the view that this is a positive and essential philosophy to adopt in schools. An initial meeting to explain the process – perhaps a slot at a regular staff meeting and providing staff with a brief written overview of the programme such as the one we have included in Appendix 1 – and regular staff briefings as to progress being made would all be helpful in achieving this goal.

It is important to point out, however, that it is generally only in schools where there is not an emotionally literate ethos or a willingness to embrace inclusion in all its aspects that opposition to the programme will arise. In such cases, we doubt whether this programme should be introduced as a tool to promote inclusion – at least, not until the whole-school belief systems and ethos have been identified, agreed and put into practice. It is when staff agree that all pupils have the right to be included in the school community that such interventions generally have more chance of succeeding. Also, witnessing such types of interventions making a real difference can, in turn, convince those who may have previously been sceptical, to adopt a more positive stance.

8. What happens if a group member begins to feel they can't cope in some way?

Given that a climate of trust, confidentiality and mutual respect will have been set up, group members should feel comfortable about raising any concerns or worries that they might have. However, if it is necessary, then the facilitator should provide some additional one-to-one advice and support for a group member as required. In our experience the provision of this additional support by the facilitator has definitely mitigated against pupils getting into a state of not being able to cope. However, it is obvious that all pupils in school will experience times of personal stress and difficulties and these may well impact upon their relationships with others, their ability to cope effectively and their ability to provide support to others who may also be experiencing similar problems. In such situations it may be necessary to adjust the level of responsibility and tasks allocated to that pupil within the group.

9. What happens if parents/carers of group members become anxious about their involvement?

Hopefully, if the initial contact is positive and the facilitator ensures that they are fully informed as to what the programme is all about and they are reassured that they can contact the facilitator if necessary, throughout the course of the programme, then their concerns can be minimised. However, things do go 'wrong' and no programme will run absolutely smoothly or to order. This needs to be pointed out during the initial contact with parents/carers alongside stressing the support structures that are there for their children should problems arise. If parents/carers do become anxious in this way, the facilitator should contact them and talk through their concerns and identify how these can and will be addressed. Clearly, if they remain unconvinced or worried then they may wish to withdraw their child from the group. This would obviously be the worst case scenario and can hopefully be avoided if the above described courses of action are taken.

10. Can the programme become part of the curriculum?

We strongly believe that teaching all pupils the social, emotional and behavioural skills (SEBS) they will need in order to be confident, competent and successful individuals within all social contexts should be part of the school curriculum. In the words of the National Primary Strategy guidance for Developing SEBS these skills should be taught. The ethos of inclusion and emotionally literate behaviour should also permeate every structure, system, policy and participant within the school context thus these skills should also be 'caught'. Clearly, the PSHE and Citizenship curriculum and the development of policies and resources to promote inclusion and emotional literacy can begin to ensure that all pupils can develop the SEBS that they need. This programme is clearly in line with such thinking and the philosophy and belief system that underpins it needs to permeate the schools systems and practice as a whole. However, we would not recommend that the intervention should be part of curriculum time. It is an intervention, which is best set up and run during a lunch break. It is the effects of the work done during this period that will then be felt and identified during both curriculum and non-curriculum time.

11. What other strategies can schools use to promote the inclusion of all pupils?

This is clearly a massive topic and we can in no sense hope to provide a fully comprehensive answer to this question within the confines of this book. However, we would suggest that the following strategies may help schools to further promote the inclusion of all pupils:

- An agreed policy for promoting inclusion, which is reviewed and reformulated annually.
- Facilities to ensure that students with disabilities can access equipment, rooms, resources and all activities within the school context.
- Access to social skills training.
- Mentors and support workers and counsellors.
- An emotional literacy curriculum.
- Access to anger management and problem-solving skills training.
- An alternative curriculum to engage the disaffected and those not inclined to be 'academic'.

- Individualised programmes of work for those who require this.

- Use of peer mentoring, conflict resolution, peer meditation, peer tutoring, buddy schemes, Circle Time and other tools for inclusion.

- A continued focus upon friendship and the skills of friendship via PSHE curriculum, assemblies, literature chosen within other subject areas, the use of the School Council and the school's inclusion procedures.

- On-going staff support and training in all areas of inclusive practice.

An important document on this topic, *What Works In Developing Children's Emotional and Social Competence and Wellbeing?* (DfES Research report 456, 2003, by Katherine Weare and Gay Gray) is available from The Health Education Unit, Research and Graduate School of Education, University of Southampton.

12. What qualities and skills does the facilitator need in order to run the programme?

There are a range of qualities and skills that most people who work successfully with children and students make use of on a daily basis. The facilitator will also need time dedicated not only for running the sessions but also for on-going liaison with other members of staff and parents/carers as appropriate throughout the duration of the intervention. The skills needed include the following:

- the ability to be flexible and not 'in control'
- the ability to understand group processes
- the ability to listen and to reflect
- good organisational skills
- the ability to see things in the moment
- an understanding of how behaviour is learnt and can be changed
- empathy and sensitivity towards others' feelings and situations
- self-awareness and self-knowledge
- emotionally literate and socially skilled
- the ability to feed back ideas and liaise effectively with staff, parents/carers and pupils, that is, good communication skills
- to manage personal stressors effectively and to be able to support others in managing stress
- to be committed to and actively participate in the practice of inclusion.

Bibliography

Cowie, H. & Wallace, P. (2000) *Peer Support in Action*. London: Sage Publications.

Duck, S. (1991) *Friends for Life*. Hertfordshire: Harvester Wheatsheaf.

Mercer, N. (2000) *Words and Minds*. London: Routledge.

Newton, C. & Wilson, D. (1999) *Circle of Friends*. Dunstable: Folens Publishers Ltd.

Pearpoint, J., Forest, M. & Snow, J. (1993) *The Inclusive Papers – Strategies to Make Inclusion Work*. Toronto: Inclusion Press.

Resnick, L. B. (1987) *Education and Learning to Think*. Washington: National Academy Press.

Rhodes, J. & Ajmal, Y. (1995) *Solution Focused Thinking in Schools*. London: B.T. Press.

Shaw, L. (1990) *Each Belongs – Integrated Education in Canada*. Bristol: The Centre for Studies in Inclusive Education.

Tyrrell, J. (2002) *Peer Mediation*. London: Souvenir Press.

Step 1

The Whole Class
Session

Step 1: The Whole Class Session

Preliminaries

It is essential that prior to conducting the whole class session the facilitator has distributed an information sheet to staff and held a question and answer session at a staff meeting or briefing session. See Appendix 1, a pro-forma staff information sheet.

It is also essential that a letter has been distributed to all the parents/carers of the pupils in the class informing them of the programme and giving them an opportunity to raise any concerns. See Appendix 2, a pro-forma parent/carer letter.

This session aims to firstly introduce the whole class to the programme and secondly identify the pupils (between 8 and 12) who will participate in the group. (The group will include both pupils who have high and those who have low social acceptance within the class however no distinction will be made between the pupils taking part in the programme at any point.)

Introducing the programme

The facilitator will need to open the session by explaining to the class the concept of Talk Time. In order to do this the facilitator may usefully make the following points:

- Initially, it will be important to set the context by emphasising the importance of working together to create a cooperative classroom and how everyone, at some point in their lives and for a variety of reasons may require support in order to feel included.

- It will be important to stress the extent to which everyone needs to feel respected, valued and included and how important it is that members of a class pull together as a team and all play a part in supporting each other throughout the school year.

- The facilitator will need to explain that the group is being formed in order to increase the cohesion of the class, to help all its members to get along together, be cooperative and ensure that nobody is isolated or neglected.

- The facilitator will need to explain that a range of pupils will be selected to join the group and share the responsibility for developing a cooperative class.

- Membership will not be restricted to the most academically able or well-behaved members of the class. The members of the group will be selected on the basis that they are representative of the whole class.

- The facilitator may also wish to inform the class that if the group runs for another term different pupils will be selected to take part.

- It will be important to inform the class that the group will meet weekly for about 30-45 minutes during a lunch time and that the group will run for 8-10 weeks.

- It will be important at this point to give the class an opportunity to ask any questions they may have about the group.

Selecting the group members

Although the facilitator may already know which pupils would benefit from support in order to become more fully included in the peer group and which pupils may be capable of providing it, the Relationship Circles and Friendship Quiz worksheets will provide the facilitator with additional information about the social dynamics of the class group and also confirm his judgement about who should be included in the group.

Relationship Circles

Each pupil will be asked to complete the Relationship Circles worksheet. This entails each pupil thinking about the people in their lives, family, friends and acquaintances and writing in their names in the appropriate circle on the worksheet. Before the pupils start the activity it will be helpful for the facilitator to explain each category in turn and to ensure that these numbered headings are written on a visible whiteboard as an aid to recording. The pupils are asked to think about four categories of people in their lives. They are:

1. Anchors – usually family members or carers who are the closest to them and love and care for them.

2. Friends – best friends and friends who they usually see on a regular basis and are therefore close to.

3. Acquaintances – people that they see on a regular basis in school or social contexts.

4. Paid people – those professionals who are paid to be in their lives, for example, doctor, dentist, teacher, teaching assistant, youth worker or mentor.

It will be important for the facilitator to stress to the pupils that this is an individual activity. Pupils should be encouraged not to discuss the activity with each other as they complete the task, as this may lead them to influencing each other's responses. Pupils can write or draw and label as appropriate. The process of completing the Relationship Circles should emphasise to the pupils the central role that other people, be it family or friends, play in their lives.

Relationship Circles

Complete your own Relationship Circles.
Start in the middle with your anchors and then work outwards.
Write or draw and label

Name...

Date...

PAID PEOPLE
People who are paid to help you e.g your dentist/ doctor

ASSOCIATES & ACQUAINTANCES
People you see regularly at school or outside of school

FRIENDS
Best friends

YOUR ANCHORS
People who love and
care for you

Kate (mum)
Bernard (dad)

evan and Faye

Phillip Liam Carmel Rachael Sinead Katie Alex

Seijun

Patrick Mr Thomas

The teachers and Dr Sharma

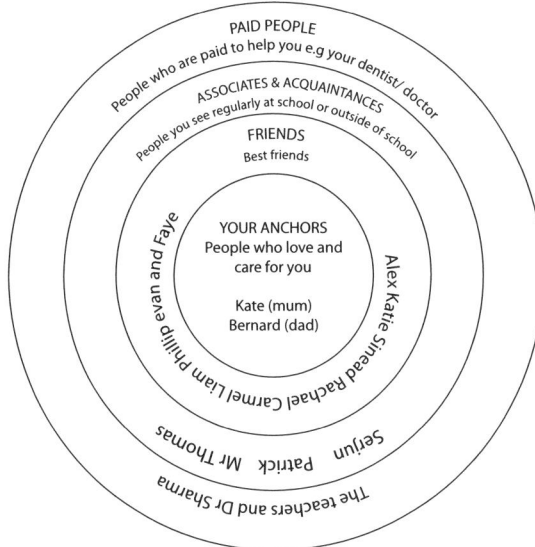

An examination of the completed worksheets after the lesson will highlight to the facilitator, the pupils who have indicated on the worksheet that they have few friends or acquaintances and thus are likely to feel neglected by their peer group, and those who have indicated, by including a number of friends and acquaintances in the appropriate circles, that they are well accepted. The facilitator may also notice that there are some 'crossovers'. For example, a number of pupils may place their class teacher or teaching assistant within the first or second circle. He will frequently be regarded by the pupil as someone who loves and cares for them and the notion of professional boundaries may be of little relevance.

The facilitator should store the completed worksheets and should ask the class to repeat the activity at the end of the programme in order to assess how the intervention has influenced the social dynamics of the class. In our experience pupils who first time round were unable to include many of the names of their peers as friends and acquaintances are now able to do so.

Brainstorming – how do they feel?

The facilitator can act as a scribe on behalf of the pupils posing the questions:

'How would you feel if some of your circles were empty?'

'How might you behave if some of your circles were empty?'

It is vital not to impose any 'adult' view at this point but to really encourage the pupils to discuss the kind of behaviour that they consider would be a consequence of feeling left out in school. Responses can be recorded on a whiteboard in two columns as in the following example:

Feelings		Behaviours	
sad	confused	crying	lying
angry	hurt	hitting	stealing
upset	unwanted	shouting	screaming
rejected	desperate	withdrawing	cheating
hated	mean	being sullen	hurting
unloved	uncertain	moody	not talking
furious	fed up	spitting	playing dumb
isolated	left out	lashing out	
mad	scared	verbally abusing	being unkind
bad	stressed	running away	being nasty
excluded	victimised	fighting	not sharing
lonely	hated	cussing	not taking turns
misunderstood	numb	hiding	not saying 'I'm sorry' or 'I'm wrong'
jealous	miserable		

This activity should begin to highlight and reinforce the connection between feelings and behaviours, and help the pupils gain an understanding of how our underlying needs may be expressed. Identifying and labelling feelings in both themselves and others and understanding how these impact upon behaviour are life skills that all pupils need to develop if they are to manage both themselves and their relationships effectively. What should also be highlighted by the facilitator at this stage, is the fact that even if someone is feeling excluded and behaving in a negative way, this does not mean that they have lost their inherent ability to change – far from it – and in setting up any kind of intervention of this kind, we are reconfirming the possibility of change and the fact that we can all play a positive part in such a process.

Friendship Quiz

Finally in this session each pupil is asked to complete a short questionnaire in order to provide the facilitator with more specific information about the existing patterns of friendships within the class. It is particularly important for the facilitator to emphasise to the pupils the confidential nature of this activity and to reassure them that the information that they each provide will be treated in strict confidence. The Friendship Quiz asks the pupils to answer six questions:

1. If you were going on a school trip, who from your class would you most like to be your partner and why?

2. If you were going on a school trip with your class, who would you most like to sit next to on the coach and why?

3. Who from your class would you like to share a room with during the trip and why?

4. If you were going on a school trip who from your class would you not like to be your partner and why?

5. If you were going on a school trip, who from your class would you not like to sit next to on the coach and why?

6. Who from your class would you not like to share a room with during the trip and why?

Scoring the Friendship Quiz

After the whole class session the facilitator will need to score the pupils' responses to the Friendship Quiz. The facilitator will need to have a full class list available in order to score the pupils' responses. Each time a pupil is mentioned in the first three questions she should receive a tick by her name. Each time she is mentioned in questions 4 – 6 she should receive a cross by her name.

In our experience of using the Friendship Quiz we have found that in each class there are usually approximately five pupils who receive a greater number of ticks than their peers. This group of pupils usually score in the region of 6 – 8 ticks (or positive nominations). There are also usually a smaller number of pupils (usually between 2 – 4 pupils) who receive more crosses (negative nominations) than their peers. The pupils with the highest number of positive nominations and those with the highest number of negative nominations are those who the facilitator is likely to judge as being suitable to join the group. It may also be helpful for the facilitator to cross reference the results of the Friendship Quiz with the results of the Relationship Circles and note whether the pupils with the most positive nominations in the Friendship Quiz are also those who have included many names in the friends and acquaintances categories of the Relationship Circles. It will also be helpful to check whether pupils with the most negative nominations are also those with few friends and allies in the Relationship Circles.

In selecting potential members of the group the facilitator will also need to take into account his prior knowledge of the pupils such as:

* Pupils who might benefit from being a support to others and need to further develop empathy, listening skills and problem-solving skills.

* Pupils who have strong leadership skills.

* Pupils who have the potential to lead and support others but may have channelled their energies in a negative way in the past, for example, involvement in bullying.

* Pupils who appear to be isolated from the peer group.

* Pupils who lack confidence and self-esteem.

* Looked After Children.

The group will include both pupils who know how to be attentive, helpful and approving and enjoy acceptance from the peer group and those who do not appear to be so well accepted by their peers. The facilitator will speak individually to each of the selected pupils (8-12 in total) and ask if they are willing to make a commitment to be part of a group which will operate for between 8-10 weeks (approximately a term).

The aim of the group is to develop a culture of emotional literacy – one in which a key group of pupils enhance their empathy and problem-solving skills by supporting each other in a structured way. The initial meeting of the group will clearly set this agenda whilst subsequent sessions will encourage the pupils to develop their own interpersonal skills alongside harnessing both their own and others' inherent ability to change.

Resources

The facilitator will need to ensure that the following resources are available:

• Whiteboard or flipchart for recording the pupils' responses and ideas.

• A copy of the Relationship Circles worksheet for each pupil.

• A copy of the Friendship Quiz for each pupil.

• Pencils, rubbers, sharpeners.

• Additionally the facilitator will need a copy of the class list.

Relationship Circles

Complete your own Relationship Circles.
Start in the middle with your anchors and then work outwards.
Write or draw and label.

Name..

Date..

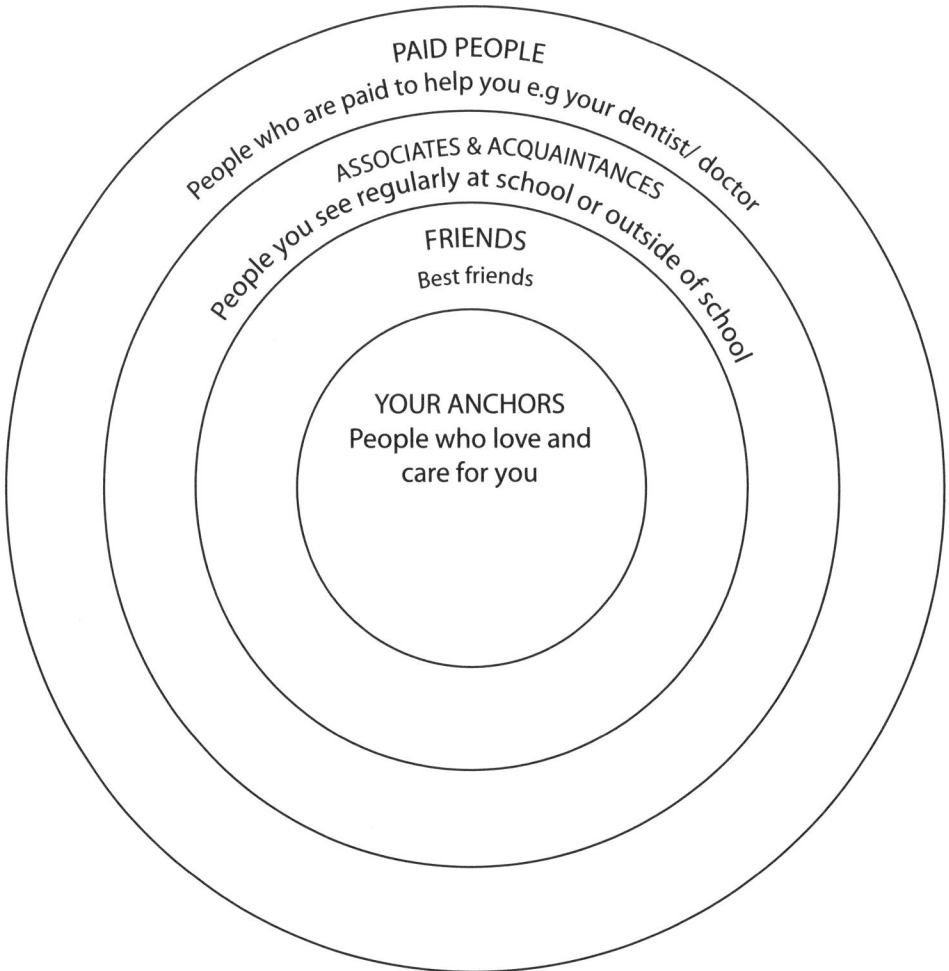

PAID PEOPLE
People who are paid to help you e.g your dentist/ doctor

ASSOCIATES & ACQUAINTANCES
People you see regularly at school or outside of school

FRIENDS
Best friends

YOUR ANCHORS
People who love and
care for you

Friendship Quiz

Name .... Date ....

Think carefully and then answer the questions.
Remember to keep it confidential!

1. If you were going away on a school trip with your class, who would you most like to be your partner and why?

2. If you were going on a school trip with your class, who would you most like to sit next to on the coach and why?

3. Who from your class would you like to share a room with during the trip and why?

4. If you were going on a school trip, who from your class would you not like to be your partner and why?

5. If you were going on a school trip, who from your class would you not like to sit next to on the coach and why?

6. Who from your class would you not like to share a room with during the trip and why?

Step 2

Setting up the Group

Step 2: Setting up the Group

Group session 1

The facilitator will, by the time of the first group meeting, have:

- introduced the programme to the whole staff

- informed parents/carers about the programme

- held the whole class session

- identified the group of pupils (8-12) who are to form the group

- briefly explained the purpose of the programme to them

- made it clear to the pupils that in volunteering their time, they are making a commitment to attend the weekly group sessions, that is, they will only be able to withdraw from the group under special circumstances.

At the first group session it would be useful to again clarify the purpose of, and agree a series of, group rules in order to protect and ensure the security of all involved. Pupils may also like to agree a name for the group and perhaps design their own logo for the individual folders and group record book.

Discussion

At the beginning of the first group session the facilitator may wish to introduce the programme by highlighting the following points:

- The importance of being able to get along with others and the need for all human beings to feel supported, loved and cared for.

- The way in which we feel can and does affect our behaviours – if people feel rejected, angry, unloved or left out then this may result in 'negative' behaviours which further reinforce and ensure a state of isolation from others and possible loneliness.

- The importance of trying to understand how others feel and think and how their life experiences may have shaped their personalities.

- How this group can work together in order to support each other.

- The way in which the sessions will be structured in order to elicit their views and strategies for solving the problems that they feel need to be addressed.

- How, in the course of this programme, they will all have the opportunity to self-reflect and to learn more about how groups work.

- The importance of keeping things confidential from the onset so as to ensure the emotional safety and security of everyone in the group.

Setting group rules

'Confidentiality' could be presented as the first group rule and the facilitator can then ask the pupils to brainstorm in order to agree and formulate their own rules. As the sessions will always involve the pupils in sharing ideas and contributing to the target setting process, the rules will need to include reference to the basic social skills of listening and turn-taking as well as sharing respect for other's views and opinions.

Rules may include the following:

- Don't brag to others about being in the group.

- Listen to others' views – even if you think they're wrong.

- Wait for your turn to talk and don't talk over others.

- Don't laugh at others' ideas or ridicule them in any way.

- Work together to try to solve problems.

- Be realistic and honest and say if some things are too hard.

- Consider how others are feeling and be kind to them.

- Always try to be cooperative and helpful – in and out of the group.

- Always seek help from a member of staff if something happens or if you hear about something that concerns you outside the group.

Rules can be recorded on the format provided and each member of the group can be given a copy to sign and keep.

Group name and logo

Pupils may wish to further forge the group's identity by formulating a name for themselves. A quick brainstorming session may result in a list of ideas, which can then be voted on. Alternatively, pupils may want to have some additional thinking time and return with their ideas at the next session. Some may also consider designing a special logo for the group. A worksheet has been provided for this purpose and pupils could take this away to complete in their own time.

Previously, pupils have chosen group names as follows:

Fabulous Friends

Talk Team

The Friendship Group

Support Circle

Trouble Spotters

'A' Team

Friendship Squad

Super Supporters

The Look Outs.

One group became known as 'Going for Gold' because this name symbolised a positive image for the pupils which embodied their belief and commitment to the purpose of the group. This group chose as its logo a gold medal which was drawn on gold card.

Focus activity: identifying positive behaviours

The aim of the final part of the first group meeting is to introduce the pupils to the concept of positive social behaviours, that is, that there are certain behaviours that enable us to get along more easily with others and although some of us may find it easy to be cooperative and thoughtful, everyone can learn how to develop better interpersonal skills once they understand what is involved. The pupils are asked to identify the behaviours which help them to get along with others. The list that is generated should be put up on a flipchart. It is likely to include behaviours such as:

- caring
- cheerful
- cooperative
- dependable
- easy-going
- generous
- helpful
- honest
- kind
- patient
- polite
- sharing
- thoughtful
- understanding.

At this early stage in the programme pupils may feel embarrassed or giggle during this discussion. Facilitators may need to deal with this response by reminding the group that the purpose of the discussion is to focus on positive behaviours and that laughter can be interpreted as a put-down. It is critical to the success of the group that the habit of paying attention to people's good strengths and qualities is established so that the ability to praise each other and those in the peer group becomes established and enables everyone's self-esteem to grow.

Take Home Activity

Each pupil in the group is then asked to choose one behaviour from the list on the previous page to look out for in the week ahead in others and to make a special effort to practise that chosen behaviour themselves. This activity is the beginning of explicitly encouraging the pupils in the group to focus on positive social behaviours and behave as role models for sociable behaviour within the class.

Future meetings

At the end of the session the facilitator should briefly explain how future Talk Time sessions will be organised and emphasise that throughout the sessions pupils will be encouraged to identify and discuss the effective skills and behaviours for getting along with others as well as understanding that finding solutions to problems is part of life. The pupils will also be encouraged to develop their own support strategies; setting and reviewing targets and problem-solving any difficulties on a weekly basis.

Recording the sessions

Individual or group records can be stored in a Talk Time folder. Pupils may wish to design their own front covers for either a group record book or for their own individual workbooks. This could be done as a Take Home Activity. A worksheet has been provided for this purpose.

Resources

The facilitator will need to ensure that the following resources are available:

- Whiteboard or flipchart for recording the pupils' responses and ideas.
- A copy of the Group Rules worksheet for each pupil.
- The worksheet for designing the Group Logo.
- The worksheet for designing the Talk Time folder.
- Pens, pencils, rubbers, sharpeners.
- A quiet, comfortable and private room.

Our Group Rules

We agree to ....
....
....

We agree to ....
....
....

We agree to ....
....
....

We agree to ....
....
....

We agree to ....
....
....

Signed..

Date ....

Our Group Logo

Signed ....

Date ....

Talk Time Folder

Step 3

Focus on Positive Behaviours

Step 3: Focus on Positive Behaviours

Group session 2

Reviewing group rules

At the beginning of each session it is important to revisit and re-enforce the group rules and allow time for the pupils to make amendments to them that they consider necessary.

Reporting back on Take Home Activity from previous session

Pupils then spend a few moments reminding themselves of the Take Home Activity from the previous session and prepare to feed back, in turn, to the group. It is important to remind the pupils that their feedback must focus on positive behaviours and not include the names of pupils who are not present in the group.

Examples of positive behaviours that pupils worked on and have reported back at this stage of the programme include:

- spending time with pupils who they do not normally play with

- encouraging more pupils to join in a playground game or discussion

- greeting and talking to all members of the class rather than restricting smiles and hello's to a selected few

- giving Christmas cards to everybody in the class

- asking the class teacher to hold a Circle Time to sort out a specific difficulty

- sharing crisps and sweets with anybody standing nearby not just with a special friend

- wishing good luck to all the pupils who are going for their high school interviews

- making an effort to include pupils who seem to be by themselves in the playground

- making an effort to choose first for team games pupils who are usually left to the end.

This structured group discussion which is carried out during each session is a critical part of the work of the group. A number of the pupils who have been identified to form the group will already know how to be attentive, helpful and approving. Such pupils are usually well liked by their peers and regarded as positive role models by staff. Their effective, interpersonal skills will hopefully be reinforced and further enhanced by their involvement in the programme. The sessions provide an opportunity for them to share their knowledge, experience and opinions with peers with whom they may not usually come into contact with and thus provide the opportunity to increase the social repertoire of the other participants. Their influence will hopefully impact positively upon the less well-accepted members of the group and in turn upon ethos and climate within the peer group and wider school community. It will be seen as 'cool' to be cooperative, to care about other's feelings and to ensure that everyone is included.

In our experience the task of the group members to model and promote pro-social behaviour gains a momentum as the weeks progress thus gradually enhancing the overall social climate of the classroom. Proximity is one of the vital antecedents of companionship and friendship and so the more often the pupils interact with each other the more likely they are to build a positive social climate within the class and ensure that everybody is included.

Focus activity and discussion

This session aims to further develop the pupils' awareness of the skills involved in getting along with others and builds on the focus on positive behaviours from the previous session. The facilitator emphasises that although some people have a talent for getting along with others and it is easy for them, for others it may be much harder. One of the purposes of the group is to examine exactly what people can do in order to get along with others. It is important that the facilitator clarifies that getting along with others does not mean that everybody will be your friend but it does mean that you will be more aware of what you can do to get along with others and thus be able to do more of these things.

What makes others like us?

It is vital that the pupils share their own ideas here and it is suggested that this activity be completed as a group brainstorm rather than on an individual basis. Pupils will tend to feel 'safer' in contributing via a generalised 'us' rather than to have to read a list of their own personal attributes.

Previous contributions have included the following:

- We smile at others.
- We know how to talk to them.
- We can get people to play with us.
- We don't hit out when we get angry.
- We can tell if someone's upset and help.
- We are clever but not boffins.
- We listen to people.
- We can say if there's a problem.
- We stick up for our friends and ourselves.
- We make an effort with our appearance.

- We don't look different so people don't laugh at us or cuss us.

- We can tell jokes.

- We feel happy most of the time.

- We can help people with work.

- We can help with problems.

- We are good at games.

- We can share stuff.

- We don't cuss people if we can help it.

Clearly many of these contributions will have engendered a good deal of discussion and questioning. For example:

- How do we really know if someone is feeling hurt or upset?

- What is 'peer pressure' and why is it so important?

- How do we control our anger?

- What do we have that makes us feel happy for most of the time?

- Why do people tease others if they look different?

There will be a wealth of issues raised, including important political and social ones, which will need to be addressed throughout the series of sessions as a whole. In our experience pupils will repeatedly return to these issues, puzzle over them and attempt to identify and formulate some answers and solutions. This discussion should be a key part of the sessions allowing pupils to articulate and reflect upon both their own skills and situations and those of the others in the group.

Why are some people less easy to get along with?

Again, this second brainstorming activity is intended as a whole-group exercise and should reinforce the distinction between the behaviours of those pupils who do have the skills and attributes to ensure their acceptance in the social network and those who don't. Pupils have previously identified the following behaviours:

- They fight.
- They hurt other people.
- They get angry too often.
- They lash out.
- They can't keep the rules in games.
- They don't listen.
- They are aggressive.
- They won't wait for their turn.

- They disrupt the lesson.
- They can't do the work and people don't want them to work on their project (in pairs/groups).
- They lie and tell on you.
- They won't admit if they are wrong.
- They cuss people all the time.
- They always look miserable.
- They can't play football.
- The teachers don't like them.
- They ruin our lessons.
- They bully you.
- They threaten people.
- They don't think about other people's feelings.
- They are too quiet.
- They don't laugh or smile.
- They look awkward.

As with the previous activity, there will be a wealth of questions and issues raised here which will clearly need to be revisited and addressed throughout the ensuing sessions. It is most important to enable the pupils to understand why some pupils are left out and have trouble getting along easily with others.

Take Home Activity

The facilitator asks the group to spend some time during the following week identifying targets that would increase their positive social behaviours and that they themselves would like to work towards achieving in the group.

Resources

The facilitator will need to ensure that the following resources are available:

- A whiteboard or flipchart for recording the pupils' responses and ideas.
- A copy (enlarged to A3 size if possible) of the Brainstorming sheet What makes others like us?
- A copy (enlarged to A3 size if possible) of the Brainstorming sheet Why are some people less easy to get along with?
- Pens, pencils, rubbers, sharpeners.
- The individual folders or group record book.
- A quiet, comfortable and private room.

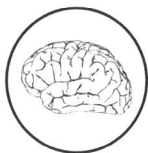

Brainstorming Sheet
What makes others like us?

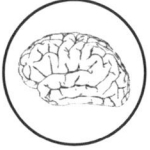

Brainstorming Sheet

Why are some people less easy to get along with?

Step 4

Taking Action

Step 4: Taking Action

Group session 3

Group rules

At the start of this group session, it will once again be important to revisit and reinforce the group rules – particularly emphasising the need for discussions within the group to remain confidential. Confidentiality is crucial at this stage when the pupils will be identifying their individual key areas for change and beginning to think about setting targets. It may also be useful to briefly revisit the two activities from the previous session: 'What makes us others like us?' and 'Why are some people less easy to get along with?'

Brainstorming sheet: What makes other like us? Observations

Each group member will have identified some specific areas of areas of change via the Take Home Activity of the previous session. The Brainstorming sheet provides a format for feedback. The facilitator may wish to enlarge this to A3 size in order to scribe for the group as a whole or may also choose to simply make use of the whiteboard using the given headings as a structure to prompt to the discussion.

During the discussion that follows the facilitator focuses with the group on specific areas of development for individual pupils. The facilitator then needs to guide each of the pupils through the stages of problem solving. At this point in the programme the facilitator may wish to use strategies such as the Miracle Question or Reframing or use the Scaling Activity worksheet (See 'Guidelines for facilitators' for guidance on using these strategies) to enable the pupils to identify their targets.

As the facilitator focuses on each individual pupil's specific area of change, the rest of the group are also encouraged to help each pupil analyse the area of development into a smaller and more manageable goal, help them to set targets to make that change and discuss what might be the longer term benefits of such change. Members of the group also agree to each take it in turns to support another member of the group over a period of a week. Each member of the group is encouraged to think:

- What could I do about this?

- How could I help?

- What could I do to make a difference to this person's goals?

What could they do about this?

The following table is an example of the areas of development which were identified in one of our programmes. (In the interests of confidentiality the names of the pupils have been changed.)

Dalila	I could stop swearing and cussing people so much.
Jason	I could stop answering back to teachers.
Raheem	I could smile a bit more and relax more, looking so scared puts people off.
Ben	I could stop getting upset when people criticize me and accept that sometimes I'm in the wrong.
Stephanie	I need to walk away and tell a teacher when people are teasing me.
Darren	I could stop irritating some of the teachers and just get on with my work.

What could we do about this?

The following table contains a list of actions identified by the group in order to support each pupil.

Dalila	Remind him not to swear or cuss (but not in front of other people).
	Tell him how he hurts people and makes people nervous about coming up to him.
	Be nice to him so he doesn't feel so angry and need to swear or cuss.
Jason	Wink to remind him to behave in class.
	Tell him it doesn't matter/it's not worth it.
	Make sure he knows how to do his homework so he doesn't feel so nervous in class.
Raheem	Sit next to him in lessons.
	Ask him to join in.
	Smile at him and tell him to relax.
Ben	Let him know we like him.
	Don't laugh at him when he does get wound up and tell others (we know who) to stop it.
Stephanie	Go round with her a lot at breaks and include her in things.
	Stick up for her a bit and tell her to do it next time.
Darren	Tell him that people will find it easier to be friendly to him if he tries not to disturb the lesson.
	Make sure he understands his work so he enjoys doing it more.

Target sheet

Once each pupil in the group has identified a group member whom they feel they can support, they can then proceed to complete the Target sheet. Where a pupil is experiencing marked difficulties in managing anger and aggression, it may be useful if all group members alternate in supporting her. If a pupil is experiencing a bereavement or similar emotional problem and exhibiting more withdrawn symptoms, it may well be more appropriate for a smaller number of group members to support her. If more than one group member is to support an individual pupil, then specific responsibilities may need to be identified and agreed. For example, two group members may be able to support Stephanie at playtimes as a pair, working together in order to help her develop assertiveness skills and to make her feel more included. It may be more appropriate (and easier for the group members to cope with) if the responsibility for pre-empting Ben's aggressive outbursts is shared out on the same kind of rota system between group members.

The Target sheet allows for each pupil to identify who they will support, what needs to change and the specific things that they can do over the coming week. An example of such a completed sheet is as follows:

My Target Pupil: Darren

What needs to change?

- Darren to ask the teacher for help if he doesn't understand the work
- Darren to show his 'unhappy face' card to the teacher when he feels that he can't sit still anymore.

What can I do?
These are my targets for this week (you may have a minimum of two targets and a maximum of three).

- I will help Darren with his work if the teacher is busy.
- Remind Darren to show his 'unhappy face' card if he feels fidgety.
- Tell Darren when he does something good.

I will review my target on Friday 15th July 2005

Signed: Sean

Date: Friday 8th July 2005

Once the pupils have completed their individual sheets, it would be helpful for the facilitator to allow time for feedback so as to reinforce the action points, alongside ensuring that all the pupils receive an appropriate level of support from the group over the ensuing week.

Finally, it will be important to stress again the importance of the confidentiality rule and to assure the pupils that they should not be alarmed or worried if things don't go as well as planned. There will obviously be the opportunity to review progress and discuss and problem-solve any concerns during the following session. Most journeys don't run absolutely smoothly or to plan – that's what makes them exciting and worth the effort of planning in the first place. If things do go wrong, they need to know that they can return to the group and gain support in order to address the problem further. This is central to the process and will be evident in all subsequent sessions.

It is important that the pupils leave the session with the positive message that they can and will make a difference – genuinely caring about your peers and their wellbeing and not accepting the exclusion of others are all positive attributes that should be encouraged and are certainly highly valued. Without these, the world would be a less healthy and happy place for everyone. It is important to emphasise to pupils that they have a real part to play in ensuring that this doesn't happen in their world.

Resources

The facilitator needs to ensure that the following resources are available:

- A whiteboard or flipchart for recording the pupil's responses and ideas.
- A copy of the Brainstorming sheet What makes others like us?   Observations enlarged to A3 size.
- A copy of the Target sheet for each pupil.
- Pens, pencils, rubbers, sharpeners.
- The individual folders or group folder.
- A quiet, comfortable and private room.

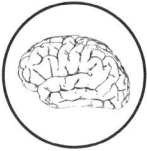

Brainstorming Sheet

What makes others like us?
Observations

What have we noticed since last week?

Name ....

Date ....

Target Sheet

My target pupil ....

What needs to change?

What can I do?

These are my targets for this week (you may have a minimum of two targets and a maximum of three).

1...

2...

3...

I will review my targets on ....

Signed ....

Date ....

Step 5

5

Reflecting and Setting Targets

Step 5: Reflecting and Setting Targets

Group session 4 onwards

Group rules

As usual, it will be important to reinforce the group rules at the start of this session prior to reviewing the pupils' progress in meeting their targets over the last weeks. The review and target setting progress, which is then introduced and utilised in this section, will continue to form the structure of subsequent sessions. The pupils will make use of the worksheets provided (Scaling Activity and Reflection and Action sheet) in order to reflect upon their progress, considering and analysing what did and didn't go well and agreeing new targets for the coming week.

The approach, which will be established by this point in the programme, is intended to be flexible and meetings can continue for as long as the pupils feel they are achieving results and making a difference. There is not a set deadline here but it is not recommended that the group continues indefinitely. We would suggest that the pupils involved agree and set their own 'end time' based upon their own feelings about their targets and their own judgements as to how they themselves are coping with supporting each other. In our experience the length of the intervention has ranged from 8-10 weeks, which usually coincides with the duration of one term. It will be important to identify and articulate success and difficulties on a weekly basis and to justify any change in focus. For example, if a pupil has clearly modified his behaviour and the number of aggressive outbursts towards others has decreased, then the group may wish to suggest he identifies a new target whilst still keeping an eye on the situation, that is, making the odd 'spot check' to ensure that all is well.

Scaling Activity

The pupils are asked to refer back to their Target sheets from the previous session and to consider how well they did in terms of meeting their targets and how things were better for their 'partner' in the group. The Scaling Activity provides a visual means of assessing progress in a solution focused way, that is, highlighting positives and negatives and prompting the question: What could I do differently in order to achieve a better outcome next week? (This question is posed as part of the Reflection and Action activity.) Pupils are presented with a scale of 1-10 and asked to award themselves a mark out of 10 for how well they feel they have done in meeting their support targets over the last week. If things have gone extremely well and they have been able to identify some significant changes or progress they may well award themselves an 8 or 9. If things have gone quite well sometimes and less well at other times then they might rate themselves at a 5 or 6. (In our experience this generally tends to be the average score at this stage in the process.) If things have gone very badly this will obviously be indicated by a much lower score. The associated difficulties will need to be further discussed within the group with everyone attempting to identify the best way forward in this particular instance.

Scaling Activity

Use a scale of 0-10 to rate your progress this week.

How well have you done meeting your support targets?

Award yourself a mark out of 10.

0 = not good   5 = OK   10 = excellent

> I have given myself a 5 because I feel : quite happy about the week but a bit sad about two things

> Things that went well were :
> I got Mel out of two fights by getting there before it got out of hand and asking her to come with me to play football and saying tocalm down and it's not worth it.

> Things that did not go so well were :
> She still had two fights that I couldn't stop and she wouldn't listen to me because she was so angry. She got told off for shouting out in maths.

Signed : Josie Read

Date : 6th June 2005

Prior to going on to the Reflection and Action activity, it is helpful to encourage the pupils to feed back and share with the group their reflections on what did or didn't go well during the past week, particularly identifying more useful strategies for the future. What is essential is that the pupils listen to each other and all have the opportunity to articulate their own ideas at this stage. The pupils need to feel confident that they can problem-solve and that their own experiences really are relevant and of value. The facilitator's role is that of an enabler – someone who can elicit the pupil's views and ideas without imposing her own views and solutions. After all, it is the pupils who are in the lessons, in the corridors, in the lunch hall and playground and they see what happens and how things can go wrong for their peers. They will also know that support and intervention from peers is far more significant for the pupils who really do 'see' and 'hear' what is going on – unlike the adults in the school context who are not part of the peer group. Consequently, we would recommend that the facilitator acts as a scribe and records any useful contributions and ideas on the whiteboard. This will aid each pupil in completing their personal Reflection and Action sheets.

Reflection and Action

This activity sheet is designed to enable each pupil to collect and order their own personal thoughts and to identify a way forward in terms of their own targets and also in their role as peer supporter. All the pupils in the group will be continually asked to reflect upon and analyse not only their own behaviours and feelings but also those of their partner in the group. The facilitator should encourage the pupils to think about their own responses, reactions and, essentially, their belief systems, that is, what made 'me' react in that way? Was it the best/right thing to do? Did I jump to conclusions? Although the questioning can be endless, the time constraints on these sessions will generally not allow for an extended debate. This is why the approach we recommend is solution focused. Naturally, although we want the pupils to develop these reflective skills and we consider that they do so throughout the programme, we also want them to be able to identify problems reasonably quickly and accurately and to make use of problem-solving questions and strategies in order to 'act' and effect change.

The Reflection and Action sheet asks the pupils to think very carefully about why things went well and why things may not have gone so well. The pupil is then asked to identify what she may do differently next time and to then set new targets for the coming week.

Reflection and Action

Reflection : Think carefully about why things went well and why they may not have gone so well. Make notes.

Notes
* I think Mel can't cope when people make her feel dumb. She gets really wound up about it because she knows she's not the best at everything. I think that's partly why she'll lash out – it's not always the other person she's angry with – it's like a build up of her anger. That's what didn't go well.

* She shouted out in Maths because she sat next to loud people. She was better in English because she sat with James and Sara.

What will you do differently next time?
I won't get so upset if she doesn't listen to me and I'll wait until later and talk to her when I can get her on her own.
I won't get so worried about it and share the responsibility with Sara.

Action: Set your new targets for the week

Target 1: To make a joke of it if other people try to cuss Mel.

Target 2: To ask her to play football with me (or another game) if she's on her own.

Target 3: To sit next to her in Maths on Mondays and Wednesday (Sara to do Tuesday, Thursday and Friday).

I will review my targets on: 13th June 2005

Signed : Josie Read

Date : 6th June 2005

What this particular example also illustrates (apart from this pupil's increasing skills of self-reflection) is the importance of support from within the group. Josie stated that she had felt upset when Mel hadn't listened to her and had been worried about her responsibility with regards to helping Mel achieve her targets. These concerns all need to be raised and addressed within the confidential group setting. Josie needs to know that it's okay to acknowledge that things may have gone wrong and that it is vital to voice her anxieties so that these can be addressed by the group. The group needs to act as a support system for its members both inside and outside the sessions thus Josie has been able to share the third target with another group member, that is, the responsibility of reminding Mel not to shout out in the Maths lessons is now shared between the two group members.

Clearly, Josie's responses are quite detailed and mature. This is a direct reflection of both her age and personality (Year 7 pupil with a mature, sensible and sensitive approach to life in general). It is important to note that the pupil's responses, and the length of time needed to record and discuss them, will vary according to the size, age and make-up of the group. The facilitator will need to judge this and pace the session accordingly. For example, a younger group of Year 5 pupils may require longer to complete the reflections and target setting process on a weekly basis as might a group of less mature Year 6 students or a fast talking, articulate and emotionally literate Year 7 group. At other times, it may be necessary to allocate some additional time but we would, however, suggest that the usual time limit should be set at around 30 minutes maximum – particularly if sessions are to run as we suggest at lunchtimes – simply to fit in with the school routine and not to cause unnecessary disruption. It is important to note that the sessions are not intended as therapy for the pupils but rather as solution focused activities, which effect changes, produce results and positive outcomes. If any individual within the group does experience particular difficulties and requires additional support then this will need to be addressed on a one-to-one basis, outside of the group time, by the facilitator.

At the end of this and each subsequent session, each pupil can be encouraged to share her targets. It is important that targets are agreed within the group and that each group member is entirely certain as to everyone else's responsibilities so that they are in a position to support and continually encourage each other in addressing their own targets and also in the job of being a peer supporter. Naturally, the encouragement to continue doing a good job and to ensure that others are included due to their actions and interventions needs to also come from the facilitator prior to the end of this and each subsequent reflecting and setting targets session.

Resources

The facilitator will need to ensure that the following resources are available:

- A whiteboard or flipchart for recording the pupils' responses and ideas.
- A copy of the Scaling Activity for each pupil.
- A copy of the Reflection and Action sheet for each pupil.
- Pens, pencils, rubbers, sharpeners.
- The individual folders or group folder.
- A quiet, comfortable and private room.

Scaling Activity

Use a scale of 0-10 to rate your progress this week. How well have you done meeting your support targets?

Award yourself a mark out of 10.

0 = not good   5 = OK   10 = excellent

I have given myself a   because I feel:

Things that went well were:

Things that did not go so well were:

Signed ....

Date ....

Reflection and Action

Reflection: Think carefully why things went well and why they may not have gone so well. Make notes.

Notes

What will you do differently next time?

Action: Set your new targets for the week

Target 1:

Target 2:

Target 3:

I will review my targets on:

Signed:

Date:

Step 6

Evaluation

Step 6: Evaluation

Final group session

In this final session, the group will have the opportunity to evaluate the work that they have done and any impact that they have had in terms of achieving their targets and providing support to each other. The pupils will also be encouraged to identify any further changes or strategies that may need to be put into place in the future and have the opportunity to consider and articulate the range of skills, strategies and ideas that they have learnt from the sessions. Most importantly, the positive, inclusive pro-social nature of this work should be celebrated and each member of the group rewarded for having participated in this programme.

Final Scaling Activity

The pupils are asked to refer back to their Target sheets from the previous sessions and to consider how well they did overall in terms of meeting these targets over the whole period, that is, however many weeks the group ran for. As always, this Scaling Activity provides a means of assessing progress in a solution focused way, that is, highlighting the positives and identifying areas for future work. Pupils should be entirely comfortable with this rating process at this stage and have no difficulty in awarding themselves a mark out of 10 for how well they feel they have done in meeting their targets. If they feel that they have really made quite a positive and significant impact then they may well award themselves an 8 or a 9. Scores will decrease if they feel that their impact has been less successful. It is hoped that the support in the group and the joint problem-solving process used will have pre-empted the lowest scores from continually appearing, that is, if pupils felt that things were negative on a weekly basis, this would have been picked up and dealt with by the group members and the facilitator.

Reflect and Review

Once pupils have had the opportunity to verbally feed back on the Scaling Activity, they can next complete the Reflect and Review sheet for their partners in the group. The pupils are asked once again to reflect and analyse the progress of their partners and to identify strategies which have been successful, different types of support and specific targets for the future.

An example of a completed sheet is as follows:

Reflect and Review

Name of partner: Alex Heath

What has changed and what has gone well?
- He is in fewer fights in the playground.
- People have stopped cussing him as much.
- He can walk away sometimes and won't always get involved in cussing them back.

What strategies worked best?
- Asking him to come and play football when things weren't going well.
- Being kind to him.

What didn't work so well?
- Telling him to leave the situation when he'd already lost it because he took it out on us then.
- He couldn't walk away when they were racist and it didn't matter what we said to him.

What needs to change further? What strategies, support and targets do you suggest for the future?
- Buddies to watch out for him, play with him and be there for him to talk to if he gets mad.
- A target for him to walk away before his anger takes control.

Thank you for your help and support.

The pupils can be given the opportunity to feed back on this activity and it will be necessary for the facilitator to also ensure that arrangements are made to feed back to staff and parents/carers as appropriate, subsequent to this final meeting of the group. The pupils need to know that what they have done has been important and has made a difference.

The Friendship Quiz and Relationship Circles from Step 1 can be repeated. These could be used to monitor the changes that have occurred over the course of the programme. This is an optional activity and might not be necessary in the light of the other evaluation activities undertaken.

Final Brainstorm

(The sheet can be enlarged to A3 size and the facilitator can act as a scribe for the pupils' ideas.) This final group brainstorming activity is actually intended to boost the self-esteem of all involved in the sessions by identifying the skills, strategies and ideas that pupils have gained from the programme. In attempting to support others, they will not only have identified their own skills in many areas, for example, making and sustaining supportive partnerships, pre-empting conflicts, developing empathy and reading body language, but they will also have discussed new concepts and ideas with their peers and with the facilitator. These need to be articulated and celebrated.

Final Brainstorm

Stop, Think and Reflect!
What skills, strategies and ideas have we
learnt from our Talk Time sessions?
Share your views!

- How to tell if someone is getting angry by their voice and body language.
- To count to 10 and do deep breathing and to stop and think before acting if you are getting mad.
- No-one is perfect and no-one has the right to try and make anyone be perfect.
- Most people need friends. If they don't, they will feel unhappy and lonely.
- Everyone can change. If there's something wrong, you can make it better bit by bit.
- Some bullies need help too. They are unhappy and should be helped to stop.
- Solving problems is easier if you listen to each other.
- To look at myself and be honest about how I feel.
- Teachers like it if you say sorry like you really mean it and as if you're listening – I've learned how to do this and it saves a lot of bother.
- If you can't wait for your turn, people won't want to play with you.
- People should care about each other and ask why others need to cuss people – what is wrong with them that they need to hurt people?
- You don't have to be obvious about including someone in a game.
- Telling the truth sometimes hurts.
- People shouldn't be nasty about how you look but you should make the best of what you've got.
- Everyone's self-esteem needs to be good.

Certificates

Finally, the facilitator can present each pupil with a certificate, which celebrates their successful participation in the group. Also, by way of thanks, we would strongly recommend that refreshments should be made available (chocolate biscuits, crisps, fruit and so on) and some additional time allocated to allow for the pupils to really mark the occasion. The message that each pupil can continue to make use of their interpersonal skills to ensure the inclusion of others, alongside the fact that this really is a responsible and positive way to operate, needs to once again be reinforced by the facilitator.

Resources

The facilitator will need to ensure that the following resources are available:

- A whiteboard or flipchart for recording the pupils' responses and ideas.

- A copy of the Final Scaling Activity for each pupil.

- A copy of the Reflect and Review sheet for each pupil.

- A copy of the Final Brainstorm sheet enlarged to A3 size for the facilitator to use in scribing pupils' responses and ideas.

- A certificate for each group member. These will need to be photocopied onto card (A4 size) and completed by the facilitator prior to the start of this final session.

- Pens, pencils, rubbers, sharpeners.

- The individual folders or group record book.

- A quiet, comfortable and private room.

Optional

- Friendship Quiz.

- Relationship Circles.

Final Scaling Activity

Use a scale of 0-10 to rate your progress this week. How well have you done meeting your support targets?

Award yourself a mark out of 10.

0 = not good   5 = OK   10 = excellent

I have given myself a   because I feel:

Things that went well were:

Things that did not go so well were:

Signed ....

Date ....

Reflect and Review

Name of partner ....

What has changed and what has gone well?

What strategies worked best?

What didn't work so well?

What needs to change further? What strategies, support and targets do you suggest for the future?

Thank you for your help and support!

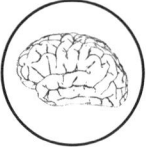

Final Brainstorm

Stop, Think and Reflect!

What skills, strategies and ideas have we learnt from our Talk Time sessions?

Share your views!

Certificate

This certificate is awarded to

....

For successfully participating in Talk Time.

Well done and congratulations!
You have made a real difference.

Thank you

Signed ....

Date ....

Friendship Quiz

Name ....

Date ....

Think carefully and then answer the questions.
Remember to keep it confidential!

1. If you were going away on a school trip, who would you most like to be your partner and why?

2. If you were going on a school trip with your class, who would you most like to sit next to on the coach and why?

3. Who from your class would you like to share a room with during the trip and why?

4. If you were going on a school trip, who from your class would you not like to be your partner and why?

5. If you were going on a school trip, who from your class would you not like to sit next to on the coach and why?

6. Who from your class would you not like to share a room with during the trip and why?

Relationship Circles

Complete your own Relationship Circles.
Start in the middle with your anchors and then work outwards.
Write or draw and label.

Name...

Date...

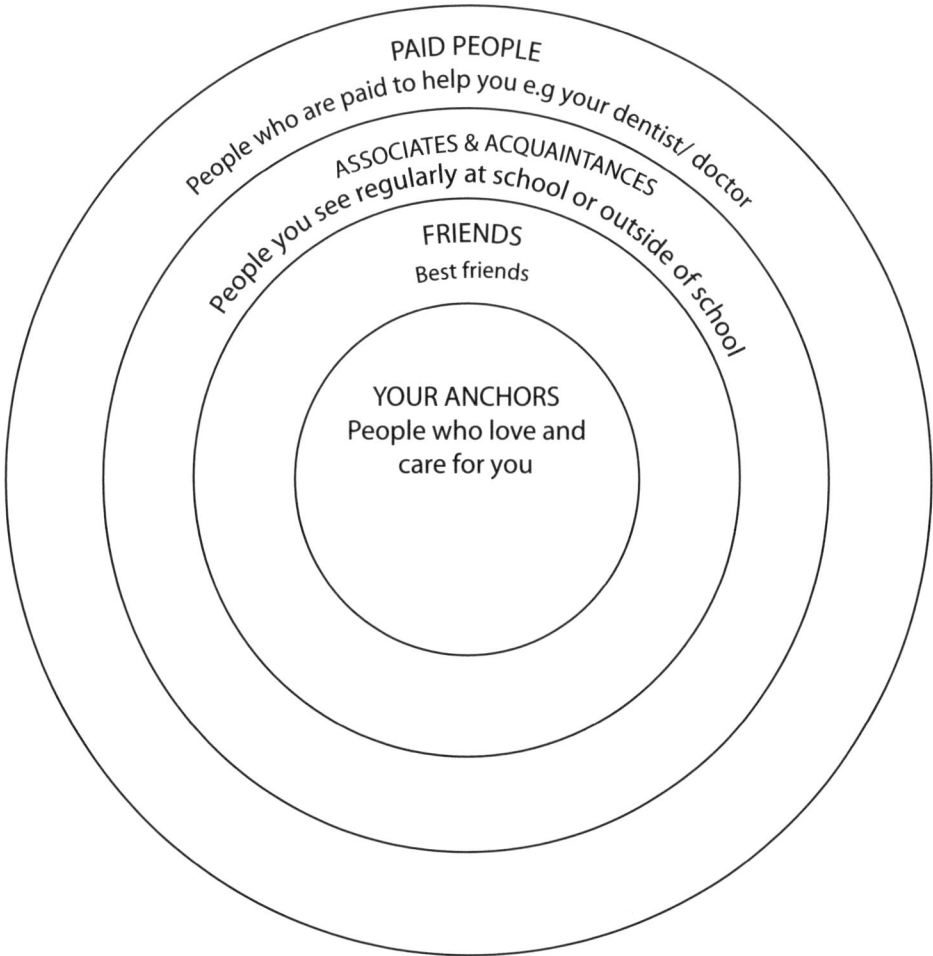

PAID PEOPLE
People who are paid to help you e.g your dentist/ doctor

ASSOCIATES & ACQUAINTANCES
People you see regularly at school or outside of school

FRIENDS
Best friends

YOUR ANCHORS
People who love and
care for you

Appendix 1: Information Sheet for Staff

An intervention called Talk Time is being introduced into our school in class ....
from .... This is a peer support programme, which will involve a group of pupils
from the class meeting together on a weekly basis for the duration of approximately
one term for 30 minutes during the lunch hour. The purpose of the group is to enable
the pupils to enhance their social effectiveness through a process of target setting.
Pupils who have been specifically selected to take part in the programme will support
each other in this process. The programme is based on the Circle of Friends approach
and the overall aim is enhance the social climate of the classroom and create a more
positive and cooperative working environment for all pupils.

The main aims of the programme are:

- to increase the level of acceptance and inclusion of pupils who are currently deemed
  to be excluded from the peer group

- to harness and further develop the skills of students who are already considered
  to be highly skilled in terms of providing friendship and support to others

- to encourage staff to reflect upon their own views and practices in order to develop
  more inclusion approaches, resources and policies

- to impact positively upon whole-school structures and systems via encouraging a
  review by the school community as to how these can be made more inclusive

- to promote a cultured ethos of social support which encourages all staff
  and students to utilise and develop their own skills in terms of valuing and
  supporting others

- to encourage the continued and on-going use of 'support teams' in order to
  ensure the inclusion of all pupils in the school context

- to further develop the social and emotional skills of those pupils identified as
  members of the group, for example, the ability to listen, to reflect, to evaluate,
  to empathise, to problem solve, to understand, identify and cope effectively with
  feeling (of self and others).

The success of the intervention will be measured by these aims.

There will be an opportunity to discuss the programme at the staff meeting on...................
If you have any questions please bring them to this meeting. Regular updates to staff
on the programme will also be provided at staff meetings.

If you require any further information, have any questions or would like to be involved
in the programme please let me know.

Programme Facilitator

Appendix 2: Information Letter for Parents/Carers

Dear Parent/Carer,

I am writing to let you know about a new programme which will be introduced in your child's class on .... The programme is called Talk Time. It will be firstly introduced to the whole class and then involve a group of between 8-10 pupils meeting weekly with myself for 30-45 minutes at lunchtime during next term. It is called a peer support programme which means the pupils meet together and support each other in developing a wide range of social and problem-solving skills under my supervision. A range of pupils will be selected to take part in the group.

The aim of the programme is to encourage the pupils to help the school to develop a more cooperative and caring classroom and one in which all the children feel supported by each other.

If you have any questions or would like any more information about the programme please let me know, I would be happy to meet with you. Appointments to see me can be made through the school secretary.

If I do not hear from you by .... I will understand that you are happy for your child to take part in the programme as a member of the small group if he/she is selected.

Yours sincerely,

Programme Facilitator

More Books from Tina Rae

Supporting Young People Coping with Grief, Loss and Death
Tina Rae

This book has been derived from the authors research and practical work with teenagers. It focuses on the development of an emotional vocabulary, empathy, tolerance and resilience.

2006 • 128 pages
Hardback (1-4129-1311-X)
Paperback (1-4129-1312-8)

Teaching Anger Management and Problem-solving Skills for 9-12 Year Olds
Tina Rae and Brian Marris

Includes sessions built around letters from a fictional character, Daniel, allowing the participants to address typical difficulties safely.

2006 • 80 pages
Paperback (1-4129-1935-5)

Good Choices
Teaching Young People Aged 8-11 to Make Positive Decisions about Their Own Lives
Tina Rae

Provides materials to teach a course on decision making for young people aged 8-11.

2006 • 128 pages
Hardback (1-4129-1818-9)
Paperback (1-4129-1819-7)

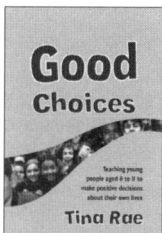

Developing Emotional Literacy with Teenage Girls
Developing Confidence, Self-Esteem and Self-Respect
Tina Rae, Lorna Nelson and Lisa Pedersen

This 10-session programme creates an opportunity for teenage girls to be clearer and more positive about their developing identities as young women.

2005 • 96 pages
Hardback (1-4129-2049-3)
Paperback (1-4129-1905-3)

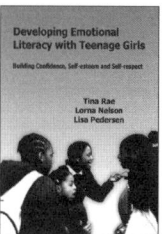

Problem Postcards
Social, Emotional and Behavioural Skills Training for Disaffected and Difficult Children aged 7-11
Janine Koeries, Brian Marris and Tina Rae

This 14-session programme is to assist young people who are disaffected and difficult, and could be at risk of exclusion.

2005 • 132 pages
Paperback (1-4129-1074-9)

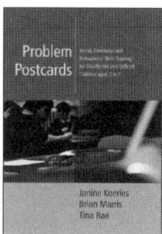

Mighty Motivators
Resource Bank for Setting Targets and Rewarding Pupil Progress at Key Stage 1 & 2
Claire Moore and Tina Rae

Contains 296 printable worksheets on a CD-ROM which encourage teachers, parents or carers, and children to work together to promote positive attitudes to learning and behaviour.

2004 • 76 pages
Paperback (1-4129-1075-7)

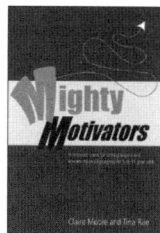

Remembering
Providing Support for Children Aged 7 to 13 Who Have Experienced Loss and Bereavement
Lorna Nelson and Tina Rae

This resource provides a range of sensitive, positive and emotionally literate activities.

2004 • 92 pages
Paperback (1-904315-42-9)

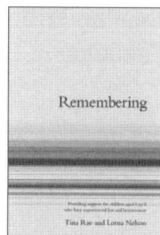

Escape from Exclusion
An Emotionally Literate Approach to Supporting Excluded and Disaffected Students at Key Stage 2, 3 and 4
Brian Marris and Tina Rae

This 15 session emotional literacy programme assists students who are disaffected and at risk of exclusion in mainstream schools.

2004 • 156 pages
Paperback (1-904315-34-8)

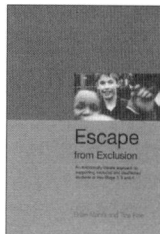

Emotional Survival
An Emotional Literacy Course for High School Students
Tina Rae

The 20 lessons explore a range of feelings and provide facilitator notes and activities to help young people develop emotional literacy.

2004 • 164 pages
Paperback (1-904315-29-1)

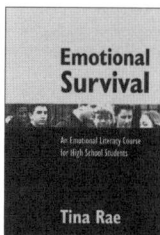

The Anger Alphabet
Understanding Anger - An Emotional Development Programme for Young Children aged 6 to 11
Tina Rae and Karen Simmons

The 26 elements of this programme help children understand anger and to see that it is linked with other feelings such as fear, loss and jealousy.

2003 • 174 pages
Paperback (1-87394-269-9)

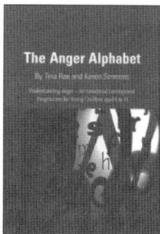

More Books from Tina Rae

Dealing with Feeling
An Emotional Literacy Curriculum
Tina Rae
This pack of materials encouraging pupils to conduct an inner dialogue, make use of a stepped approach to solving problems, and attempt to control certain impulses.
1998 • 186 pages
Paperback (1-87394-232-X)

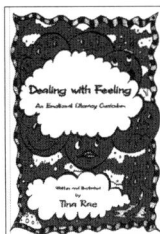

Dealing With Some More Feelings
An Emotional Literacy Curriculum for Children Aged 7 to 12
Book and CD
Tina Rae
Introduces 20 emotions ranging from possessive, sorry, guilty to helpful, brave and loyal in 20 whole class sessions.
2003 • 188 pages
Paperback (1-904315-03-8)

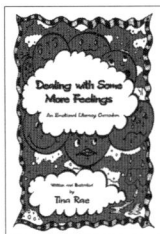

Keep Your Cooooooool!
Stress Reducing Strategies for Key Stage 2 and 3
Book and CD
Tina Rae and George Robinson
'Would be a useful resource to encourage the inclusion of emotional literacy to a wider audience without "giving away" the psychology' - *Educational Psychology in Practice*
2002 • 64 pages
Paperback (1-87394-293-1)

Peter Punk
Developing Self-Esteem, Citizenship, PSHE and Literacy Skills in the Literacy Hour for Key Stages 1 and 2
Sian Deane and Tina Rae
This programme includes lesson learning intentions, stories, questions, comprehensive teacher notes, differentiated activity sheets, follow-up suggestions, cross-curricular links and plenary questions.
2002 • 276 pages
Paperback (1-87394-279-6)

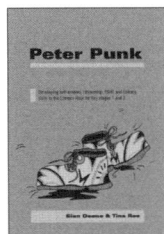

School Survival
Helping Students Survive and Succeed in Secondary School
Chris Wardle and Tina Rae
Suggests practical ways to approach difficult students that may help ensure their inclusion in the mainstream context.
2002 • 140 pages
Paperback (1-87394-229-X)

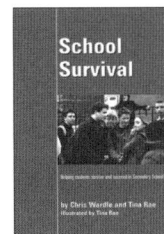

Strictly Stress
Effective Stress Management: A Series of 12 Sessions for High School Students
Tina Rae
An ideal 12 session resource for helping students understand, acknowledge and cope with specific stressors.
2001 • 134 pages
Paperback (1-87394-214-1)

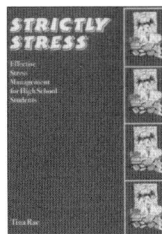

Confidence, Assertiveness, Self-Esteem
A Series of 12 Sessions for Secondary School Students
Tina Rae
This 12-session course teaches skills and strategies for more effective relationships and interactions at home and in school.
2000 • 182 pages
Paperback (1-87394-297-4)

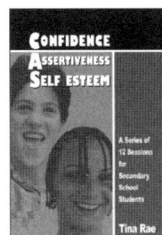

Positive People
A Self-Esteem Building Course for Young Children (Key Stages 1 & 2)
Claire Moore and Tina Rae
'This handbook is likely to be a very excellent addition to resource materials available for primary phase teachers to build on their knowledge of circle time and self-esteem activities' - *Educational Psychology in Practice*
2000 • 164 pages
Paperback (1-87394-292-3)

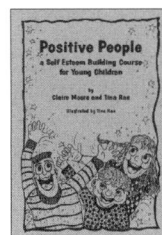

Purr-fect Skills
A Social Skills Programme for Key Stage 1
Tina Rae
'Anyone who is committed to the development of the whole child will welcome this resource' - *SNIP*
2000 • 200 pages
Hardback (1-87394-218-4)

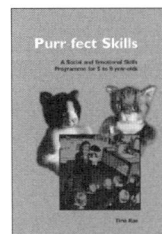

Crucial Skills
An Anger Management and Problem Solving Teaching Programme for High School Students
Penny Johnson and Tina Rae
This 10 session programme helps students aged 11 to 16 deal with and manage their anger.
1999 • 98 pages
Paperback (1-87394-267-2)

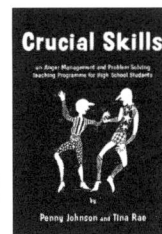

www.luckyduck.co.uk

www.paulchapmanpublishing.co.uk PCP